# Home Sweet Neighborhood

## TRANSFORMING CITIES ONE BLOCK AT A TIME

### MICHELLE MULDER

ORCA BOOK PUBLISHERS

**Library and Archives Canada Cataloguing in Publication**

Mulder, Michelle, 1976–, author
Home sweet neighborhood: transforming cities
one block at a time / Michelle Mulder.
(Orca footprints)

Includes bibliographical references and index.
Issued in print and electronic formats.
ISBN 978-1-4598-1691-6 (hardcover).—ISBN 978-1-4598-1692-3 (pdf).—
ISBN 978-1-4598-1693-0 (epub)

1. Community development—Juvenile literature.  2. City and town
life—Juvenile literature.  3. Quality of life—Juvenile literature.  4. Social
action—Juvenile literature.  5. Child volunteers—Juvenile literature.

I. Title.  II. Series: Orca footprints

HD49.C6M852019          j307.1'4          c2018-904695-3
                                          c2018-904696-1

Library of Congress Control Number: 2018954157
Simultaneously published in Canada and the United States in 2019

**Summary**: Part of the nonfiction Footprints series for middle readers,
illustrated with many color photographs. Readers will learn how to take an
active part in creating the kind of cities they'd like to live in.

*Orca Book Publishers is dedicated to preserving the environment and has
printed this book on Forest Stewardship Council® certified paper.*

Orca Book Publishers gratefully acknowledges the support for
its publishing programs provided by the following agencies:
the Government of Canada, the Canada Council for the Arts
and the Province of British Columbia through the
BC Arts Council and the Book Publishing Tax Credit.

Cover images by Jill Watt, Luke Jerram
Back cover images (top left to right): dreamstime.com, dreamstime.com,
wikimediacommons.org; (bottom left to right): dreamstime.com,
Michelle Mulder, Jenn Playford

Edited by Sarah N. Harvey
Design and production by Teresa Bubela and Jenn Playford

ORCA BOOK PUBLISHERS
orcabook.com

Printed and bound in Canada.

22  21  20  19  •  4  3  2  1

For my neighbors, with thanks.

# Contents

## CHAPTER ONE:
## THE KID NEXT DOOR

## CHAPTER TWO:
## PARTYING IN THE STREETS

# CHAPTER THREE: A POTLUCK OF POSSIBILITIES

# CHAPTER FOUR: LIFE IN THE CITY

# Introduction

Garden boxes and a bench aren't the only things we put in our parking lot. Here I am with our new book exchange. GASTÓN CASTAÑO

With imagination, even autumn raking can bring neighbors together. This leaf pile gave the kids in our building a whole week of fun. MICHELLE MULDER

Have you ever seen something so unexpected that you stopped in the middle of the sidewalk for a closer look? Maybe it was a tree fort or a giant sunflower. I love quirky details like these, but I didn't give them much thought until my own quirkiness caused a commotion in my apartment building.

My husband and I don't own a car, so we used our parking spot to grow tomatoes...which really upset one of our neighbors. Gardening encourages conversations, she said, and she didn't want extra noise outside her window. At first I was baffled—I'd planted tomatoes for salads, not for conversations—but in the years since she left our building, I've realized she was right. Gardening in shared spaces *does* spark conversation. Every time I'm outside digging, neighbors stop to chat. And I love it.

Recently I learned that there's a name for activities like these. *Placemaking* is an international movement dedicated to making neighborhoods more personal and changing outdoor spaces to draw people together. Kids are natural placemakers, building tree forts, setting up lemonade stands and chalking hopscotch squares onto sidewalks. Now adults are getting into the act too. Families around the world create book exchange boxes to trade books with passersby. In the Netherlands, people drag sofas and tables into the street to eat with neighbors. Families in Toronto, Canada, helped build a brick oven in a park so people could bake bread together. Can small, creative changes really transform entire neighborhoods? Grab a friend and come see for yourself!

In my hometown we're allowed to garden on the grassy strip between the sidewalk and the street. More space for veggies and chats with neighbors. MICHELLE MULDER

# My Happy Place

For a few days every summer, our building gets too hot for comfort. Until recently, sitting outside meant choosing between the noise of a busy street in the front or the heat of the pavement behind. So this year we all voted to put the "park" back into "parking lot." We turned one corner into a sitting area with a bench and a little lending library, and now my husband's scheming to buy a communal barbecue.

From parking lot to community gathering place—now that's a reason to celebrate!
MICHELLE MULDER

## CHAPTER ONE

# The Kid Next Door

## HELP! NEIGHBORS WANTED!

What do you do when, halfway through making pancakes, you run out of eggs? Some of us might go next door to borrow a few, but what if you don't know your neighbors?

Not long ago, talking to the neighbors was an important part of daily life, but these days, especially in big cities, it's less and less common. Many people, from psychologists to environmentalists, say that knowing our neighbors is one of the healthiest things we can do, for ourselves and for the planet—and they're thinking about more than those delicious pancakes! Biologists believe humans are designed to be happiest when living in strong communities. To see what I mean, let's take a trip back through time to see how our ancient ancestors felt about the folks next door.

*Score! This neighborhood soccer game is in Makuyu, Kenya.*
PHOTO BY BELLE MALUF ON UNSPLASH

*Steps like these ones in Bhaktapur, Nepal, can be a great place to chat with neighbors (or to rest when you're dog-tired).* ZZVET/DREAMSTIME.COM

## THE NEXT CAVE OVER

*Homo sapiens* (as we humans are known) first appeared in Africa about 200,000 years ago. For most of our existence we've lived in communities made up of only a few families. We didn't stay in one place but instead followed our food. Parents, aunts and uncles taught children where to get a good bellyful of berries in spring or an antelope drumstick in summer. Kids also learned which animals to stay away from and which to eat, how to find clean water and how to make tools.

With so much traveling, humans didn't often build permanent houses. Instead, they used natural shelters like caves or created shelters out of what was available, from a hole in the ground to animal-skin tents. Sometimes family groups stopped for a few days or even a few weeks if food was plentiful. Occasionally they'd meet up with other humans—maybe at the same fishing hole every summer—but always, each family group packed belongings (and younger siblings) onto their backs and headed off in search of the next meal.

*For thousands of years, Arctic peoples have built* inuksuit *to mark travel routes, fishing areas, camping spots, hunting grounds and food caches.* SHARPLY_DONE/ISTOCK.COM

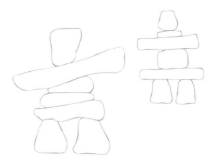

*In New York City in 1900, streets were for people, horses and vegetable-sellers. No one expected to get anywhere fast.*
LC-D401-12683/LIBRARY OF CONGRESS

## THE WORLD'S FIRST NEIGHBORS

About 12,000 years ago a few people in the Near East (western Asia) noticed that clearing space around their favorite plants and watering them made everything grow better. Eventually some families could grow enough food to survive without traveling at all. Other families joined them, and for the first time ever, people lived not just with relatives but also with folks they weren't related to at all.

Over the generations, farmers got better and better at growing food. When they regularly produced more than their own families could eat, other families in the community could stop growing food and focus instead on making shoes or wooden carts or pots to cook with. Each family traded what they made for what they needed.

About 6,000 years ago, settlements in Mesopotamia (an area that presently includes parts of Iraq, Iran, Syria and Turkey) got so big that not everyone knew each other. Important jobs

## *My Happy Place*

*When I lived in the small town of Pamparomas, Peru, I only ever saw two automobiles on the street. One was the priest's pickup truck, and the other was a van that carried passengers from village to village. No one else could afford a car, and this meant that people gathered in the streets to talk, sell things or haul cargo on their donkeys. Every afternoon our neighbors strung a volleyball net across the road in front of my friend's place. Sometimes we had to stop playing to let a donkey through, but the truck and the van drivers knew better than to interrupt our games, and they chose a different route.*

*In Pamparomas, Peru, in the year 2000, the street was for talking, walking and playing volleyball.*
MICHELLE MULDER

like building roads couldn't be organized between neighbors anymore, so communities developed governments and taxes to pay for public projects. Cities were born.

## RICH CITY LIFE

Not everyone on the planet decided to stay in one place. Indigenous people across the globe often continued to live *nomadically*. Those who chose to settle down though—in a city or in the countryside—generally grew up and lived close to where they were born. Travel was too difficult. For one thing, you had to have enough money saved up to pay for everything you'd need along the way. For another, you'd have to leave behind everyone you knew to travel through unfamiliar places (without cell phones and helpful wayfinding apps). If disease or accident struck, who would you turn to if everyone you knew was still at home?

Then, 300 years ago, something happened in Europe that made leaving home seem like a good idea after all. By 1775 a Scottish man named James Watt had developed a steam engine that could make other machines run faster than ever before. Suddenly, many of the items that people had made by hand (like cloth, for example) could be machine made. Factories began popping up in cities all over Europe, and factory owners offered workers something they'd only ever dreamed of—a regular income.

For many farmers, this looked like a golden opportunity. When beetles or a bad storm hit their crops, everyone faced starvation. But with a regular income from factory work, parents could put food on the table no matter what the weather or the local insects were doing. Sure, families would have to leave behind land where their ancestors had lived for hundreds of years. They'd say goodbye to everyone they'd ever known too. But they hoped a steady income would make it all worthwhile.

Families around Europe swapped the countryside for tiny rooms in the city and took factory jobs for the whole family,

Imagine working 12 hours each day, spinning cotton in a factory. Some of these workers were about seven years old!
LEWIS HINE/ U.S. NATIONAL ARCHIVES/WIKIPEDIA.ORG

**NEIGHBORHOOD FACT:**
Most species need thousands of years of evolution to adapt to a new environment, but not humans. We can learn how to live in new climates and environments within just a few months or years, and by 10,000 years ago, human communities existed on every continent except Antarctica.

11

even the kids. Instead of spending their days outdoors, planting and harvesting with family and neighbors, people (including children) spent twelve to nineteen hours a day in dark, noisy factories with other workers. And by the time they arrived home at night, they were exhausted and had little energy left to spend time with family and neighbors.

## PLAYING IN THE STREET

City life did get better after a while. Families adjusted to the new lifestyle, and they made friends in their neighborhoods. Overflowing from their tiny rooms, they met up outside, mostly on the street.

City streets in the 1800s were very different from the ones we know now. Out in the street you were as likely to find a donkey pulling a cart as a group of kids playing a game with sticks and stones, or a neighbor selling vegetables in front of his house. Animal poop and garbage dotted the road, and when a horse and carriage sped through, everyone dashed for safety.

In the early 1900s, all that began to change. A new invention called the automobile showed up, and this speedy vehicle was

*This was riding in high style in 1905. Pedestrians, beware!*
NA-1824-1/GLENBOW.ORG

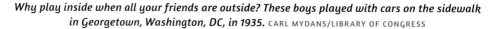

*Why play inside when all your friends are outside? These boys played with cars on the sidewalk in Georgetown, Washington, DC, in 1935.* CARL MYDANS/LIBRARY OF CONGRESS

causing accidents. At first people were furious with the drivers. At the scene of an accident, passersby would mob the car and yell at the people inside. The law came down hard on drivers too, and if someone was killed in an accident, drivers were charged with both dangerous driving and manslaughter.

Automobile owners felt frustrated. They had paid plenty of money for their cars and believed they should be free to go fast. Automobile manufacturers and car dealers agreed with drivers, and together they convinced people to buy more cars and to turn streets into car-only spaces.

## NEIGHBORS? NAH!

As years passed, people made more money, cars got cheaper and more people bought them. This meant that now people could live farther away and still get to work or school on time. These days, instead of spending almost all our time in our neighborhoods, we often spend our days somewhere else. In some places, people never even see their neighbors because they get into their cars in

*Does your city celebrate a car-free day? These kids in Milan, Italy, enjoyed theirs by playing basketball in the streets.*
PAOLO BONA/SHUTTERSTOCK.COM

# *My Happy Place*

*When I was nineteen I spent a summer volunteering in a small village in the Dominican Republic. During the week our team helped dig trenches for a water pipeline, and on weekends we walked down the mountain to swim in the river. On our way back, kids ran to meet us, calling our names. Adults heard the voices and came out of their houses to talk too. Everyone always seemed to know what was going on in El Higuito—no electricity or phones necessary!*

*When I visited, no one in El Higuito, Dominican Republic, had electricity, but word always traveled fast anyway.*
MICHELLE MULDER

*Some neighbors in the United States designate their streets as "playborhoods." These signs warn drivers to slow down.*
MIKE LANZA

*Squeeze a few lemons, spoon in some sugar, celebrate the sunshine, and meet a few neighbors!* IMAGE SOURCE/ISTOCK.COM

their garages and drive to their destinations, and when they come home they park in their garages and go right into their houses.

Cars aren't the only reason we spend less time with neighbors. A hundred years ago we *needed* our neighbors. Adults bought groceries at the neighborhood store every few days (because refrigerators didn't exist yet). And talking to neighbors was entertainment (because movies, television and the Internet hadn't been invented yet either). These days a lot of our needs can be met without leaving the house at all.

## ADVENTURE BOULEVARD

"Go outside and play!"

For a long time that was a kid's job. In summer, children would wake up, eat breakfast, do some chores and then run outside, coming home only for meals and bedtime. Parents trusted that they would be nearby and wouldn't get into mischief (or, at least, not too much). They also knew that their kids were playing with every other kid on the street and that there were enough parents around to make sure everyone stayed out of trouble.

Tree forts, tag, hopscotch and marbles kept kids entertained long before TV arrived on the scene. With all these activities, neighborhood sidewalks were bustling places. Sometimes kids roved from house to house in packs, having a snack at one place, using the bathroom at another. Kids picked up news from each family, and when they went back to their own houses, they shared it with their parents. When someone was sick, kids were often the first to report the news at home, and adults would head down the street to lend a hand with whatever needed doing. Kids played an important part in keeping neighborhoods neighborly.

## KID POWER!

What does it mean to be "connected"? For some people it means being in touch with hundreds of people online. Psychologists point out, though, that humans need strong in-person connections too. We can't rely on online friends to make us soup when we're sick, for example, or to play basketball with us.

And who are some of the world's best people at creating in-person friendships? Kids! Unlike adults, kids are more likely to *be* in a place—really *be* somewhere, without cell phones dragging their attention away from the people right in front of them, and without cars to take them somewhere else entirely. When you're not distracted, it's easier to see possibilities—like raking up a huge pile of leaves to toss yourself into, or designing an elaborate sidewalk mural with chalk. Creating something right where you are instead of waiting for someone else to create it (or going someplace where it already exists) is exciting. It's what turns *a* place into *our* place. A city begins to look like the people who live there, and we know we're home.

Placemaking is about more than making our mark. Personal touches can make life better for everyone, from reducing crime to feeding the hungry. Stroll through the next chapter to find out how.

*Sidewalks aren't just for walking and hopscotch. Why not have a little (or big) game of chess, like these kids in New York?*
LEV RADIN/SHUTTERSTOCK.COM

**NEIGHBORHOOD FACT:**
Studies show that kids who walk and bike can draw more detailed and accurate maps of their neighborhoods than those who usually ride in cars.

# My Happy Place

*A few years ago the City of Victoria turned a stretch of one of our streets into a greenway for pedestrians, cyclists and other nonmotorized folks. To mark the change, the City invited people to help paint the street. My daughter, then six, loved this project, and every time we pedal past we say hello to the part of the city we painted ourselves.*

*Here's the street that we helped paint.*
CITY OF VICTORIA

## CHAPTER TWO

# Partying in the Streets

## CHALKING UP NEW LAWS

Does hopscotch disturb neighborhood peace? And are chalk drawings on sidewalks graffiti? These were important questions in Ottawa, Ontario, in 2007 when a few kids chalked a hopscotch game on sidewalks around their city block. Adults came out to enjoy it and swap stories, but one neighbor saw the hopscotch game as *vandalism* and called the city. Soon workers showed up to scrub the sidewalks clean.

Everyone could have shrugged their shoulders and gone back inside, but instead families called their friends and told them what had happened. Before long, people throughout Ottawa were chalking their own sidewalks with "random acts of hopscotch," including a four-block trail of chalked hopscotch squares that led all the way to the front door of city hall. And guess what! Ottawa changed its graffiti laws after that. Now kids and adults alike are free to chalk sidewalks to their hearts' content.

*Who says sidewalks and roadways have to be boring gray? With permission, artists of all ages can make them beautiful!*
JENN PLAYFORD

## RIDE ON!

Hopscotch isn't the only pastime that raises eyebrows in some neighborhoods. Riding a bike can be suspect too. Even in my bicycle-friendly city I often get funny looks when people learn that I get around by bike instead of by car. To be honest, I can understand why some people think my family is strange. Victoria, like most North American cities, is designed for cars, and choosing not to have one is like showing up at a hockey game in a swimsuit and snorkel. In other words, according to some people, we use the wrong equipment for living in a city.

Not everyone agrees that cities *should* be designed for cars, though. In 2009, twelve-year-old Adam Kaddo Marino wanted to celebrate National Bike to Work Day by riding his bike to school in Saratoga Springs, New York. He and his mother pedaled together, and their arrival at school felt like a triumph...until

*Riding a bike can be a zippy way to get yourself to school.* DASHAROSATO/DREAMSTIME.COM

## NEIGHBORHOOD FACT:

What would happen if there were no cars on the road? In 2010, officials in Germany closed a road between Duisburg and Dortmund for one day, and more than 3 million people used the road to bicycle, skate and walk! This inspired Germany to build almost 100 kilometers (62 miles) of bicycle highways linking 10 German cities. The first part of the network opened in 2015.

*Streets are for artwork at this amusement park in Khao Yai, Thailand. What would the world be like if more of our streets looked like this?* P_SARANYA/ISTOCK.COM

the parking attendant, the vice-principal and then the principal laid down the law and took away Adam's bike. Walking and cycling to school had been banned in their school district since 1994 because they were too dangerous. Shocked, Adam and his mother were determined to get that rule changed. Day after day they cycled to school, not even stopping when the police were called in. It wasn't until local media heard the story that the school district made the bike ride legal. Adam's school even has a well-used bike rack now.

## WONDERFUL *WOONERVEN*

Does your family ever eat outside? If so, chances are it's on a picnic table or a blanket, but can you imagine hauling your dining-room table out into the street? It's common in the Netherlands. There, front doors often open right onto narrow sidewalks. For a long time, speedy cars terrified people whenever they stepped out of their houses. Then local families began to place furniture and plants on the street, kind of like little living rooms stretching into the area that was once only for cars.

*Most cities offer block-party permits to cut off traffic for a day. Neighbors share a meal, play games and enjoy live entertainment.*
ONEBLUELIGHT/ISTOCK.COM

*Cars won't be going fast down this Dutch street!* CANIN ASSOCIATES

The result? Much slower traffic! In fact, this approach worked so well that there are now more than 6,000 such streets—called *woonerven*, or "living streets"—in the Netherlands, and the idea has spread to many other countries.

## KNITTERS FOR SAFE STREETS

Pedaling to school, meeting your neighbors, having supper on the sidewalk (or in the street)—these all sound like lovely ideas, but what if you live in a rough part of town? At Yesler Place public housing project in Seattle, Washington, people used to stay inside to avoid the dealers selling drugs on street corners. But one group of grandmothers refused to hide away indoors. Instead, the women dragged lawn chairs to the most crime-ridden corners and started knitting. The result? The drug dealers took off and never came back. Sometimes just being on the streets—walking, sitting or even making socks—can be enough to make a neighborhood safer.

*When Svante Myrick became mayor of Ithaca, NY, he turned his official parking spot into a little park. The sign says* Reserved for Mayor and friends! PHOTO COURTESY OF THE OFFICE OF MAYOR SVANTE MYRICK

**NEIGHBORHOOD FACT:**
Many police forces say the most effective way to cut crime in a neighborhood is for neighbors to spend more time together outside.

# My Happy Place

*Not having a car, my family generally stays within easy cycling distance of home. This affects our lives in many ways. For one thing, our daughter isn't involved in many after-school activities because pedaling there and back would take too much time. But since we spend so much time in our neighborhood, we know our neighbors well, and there's always lots going on here anyway, from playtime with the other kids in our building to picnics to cartwheel contests on the sidewalk. Making our own entertainment is fun in itself!*

*Sometimes we even go camping by bicycle.* MICHELLE MULDER

*A neighborhood basketball game isn't just fun. It can make for safer streets and healthier communities too.* RUSS ENSLEY/DREAMSTIME.COM

Other times, increasing safety can be more complicated. In parts of Chicago, Illinois, gangs control public spaces, and being outside might mean getting shot. But a program called Hoops in the Hood is changing that. Every week in the summer, organizers choose a city block known for gang violence. They tell residents that they'll be closing the street for an evening, ask people to move their cars and invite kids from opposing gangs to join them for a basketball game. The street transforms from war zone to neighborhood festival, with little kids riding their tricycles around, bigger kids shooting hoops, and neighbors getting to know each other. Together, game by game, the kids are making their streets safe again.

## CHAIRS, CHAIRS, EVERYWHERE

As soon as we had a bench at the edge of our parking lot, I started meeting more people in our neighborhood. Passersby would comment on the bench or come over to ask about our garden boxes. Now that we've added a book exchange box, our street has also become a destination for avid readers. It turns out we've created what city planners call a *bumping place*—a public space where people are likely to see each other, stop and chat. Bumping places are crucial in building community, and all it took was a bit of *street furniture*.

Street furniture is changing the face of New York City as well. For decades, Times Square was one of the noisiest parts of the city, with honking cars backed up for blocks. Traffic was so slow, in fact, that many people were horrified when the city decided to block off the area to vehicles altogether. But one weekend in May 2009, barriers went up on the roads, and 376 colorful beach chairs showed up on the pavement. People flooded the street, and instead of complaining about traffic problems, local newspaper articles were all about those bright chairs and the experience of seeing the famous area from a whole different angle. These days, Times Square is permanently closed to vehicle

*New Yorkers were fascinated when they could walk—and sit—in the middle of Times Square, beginning in 2009.*
JIM.HENDERSON/WIKIPEDIA.ORG

traffic, and permanent furniture is in place. The same is happening in many other busy parts of New York City.

## POTHOLE PARKS

Seating areas aren't the only things people are building into their neighborhoods. Some people build entire parks too—right in the street!

In 2005, designers at a San Francisco art and design studio were frustrated with how much public space was reserved for parking cars. They wanted more green space, so one day they wandered out of their office, put money into a parking meter and rolled some sod (sections of lawn) over the empty parking spot. They added a tree in a pot, set up a bench and stretched out on the grass to read a newspaper. Two hours later, when the parking meter expired, they cleaned up and went back to work.

*Roll out some grass, drag over a tree and a bench, and your parking spot becomes a pleasant little park.* SALTYBOATR/WIKIPEDIA.ORG

# *My Happy Place*

*Years ago my family and I lived on a quiet dead-end street. At the end of the street was Victoria's smallest park: just a patch of grass, a tree, a bench and a flower bed. One year the city decided to cut costs by removing the flowers and planting grass instead. The tiny park looked sadder to me, and an interesting thing also happened. We noticed beer cans, cigarette butts and other trash collecting next to the bench. People began leaving old furniture there as well. The next spring the city put the flowers back, and the problem of trash and abandoned furniture disappeared entirely. Caring for a place can inspire others to care too.*

*Can planting flowers on streets help to reduce littering?*
IGOR MARUSITSENKO/DREAMSTIME.COM

21

*Ever wish people would slow down and admire the view? City officials in Paris, France, made it happen by turning this piece of expressway into a beach!* PEZI/WIKIMEDIACOMMONS.ORG

Since then San Francisco has converted several of its parking spots into permanent mini parks, and on the third Friday of every September, people in cities around the world pay local parking meters and try PARKing for themselves!

Steve Wheen of London, England, needs even less space to create his parks. For a long time he felt frustrated about many different things that didn't seem related—his neighborhood's sidewalks were full of dangerous potholes, he was a gardener without a garden, and London is dull and gray during some parts of the year. He decided to brighten things up by planting a few flowers and setting up a miniature scene in a local sidewalk pothole. He watched people's faces light up when they saw it, and that was it—Steve Wheen was hooked. He's since created hundreds of pothole gardens and inspired people all over the world to do the same.

## REALLY? HERE, IN THE CITY?

Can a pile of sand change a city? You bet!

In 2002, city officials in Paris, France, were determined to reduce car traffic. Pollution was bad, and cars zoomed past what would otherwise have been a lovely walk on the bank of the River Seine. So for part of the summer the city closed 1.2 kilometers (0.75 miles) of the Pompidou Expressway, buried it in sand and brought in palm trees, a climbing wall and ball courts. Some folks thought it was a ridiculous idea, causing more traffic problems than ever. But two million people enjoyed the riverside beach that summer, sunbathing by day and walking to nearby concerts in the evening. The creation of a beach in the middle of the expressway became an annual tradition, and in 2016, Paris closed that section to cars for a full six months to see if it could be a pedestrian paradise year-round. A little sand goes a long way!

And so do a few cans of paint. Artist Edi Rama grew up in the gray city of Tirana, Albania. Buildings were gray. The streets were gray. Litter was everywhere, and so was crime.

*Folks in Tirana, Albania, discovered that bright paint colors can make a city cheerier, reduce crime and encourage friendliness. Wow!* ALBINFO/WIKIPEDIA.ORG

23

*Neighbors on Hulbert Street, near Perth, Australia, built themselves a skateboard ramp as their first project together. They now also have a communal bike-storage unit, goats, weekly teas and an annual street festival.*
SHANI GRAHAM

*When neighbors turn an empty lot into a community garden, they can grow food... and friendships!*
SOLSTOCK/ISTOCK.COM

When Mr. Rama became mayor in 2000, he ordered large quantities of paint in wild colors, and over the next few years city workers repainted buildings throughout the city with indigo or melon-orange paint, in rainbows, stars or other shapes. Many local residents were horrified, but most said the project should continue. They'd noticed changes in the city that went much deeper than the layers of paint. Neighbors were spending more time outside, there was less litter, and shopkeepers began taking bars off windows because crime was going down.

## ENVIRONMENTAL AND FRIENDLY

Riding a bike to school, knitting on a street corner, repainting the city in bright colors—all these ideas bring a new twist to daily life, but are they worth the effort? Studies say yes. In places where neighbors know each other and spend time together, mental health challenges (like depression, anxiety and *schizophrenia*) are much less common. Scientists have even found a link between loneliness and physical sickness—the more time people spend with family, neighbors and friends, the less likely they are to get sick! Still other studies suggest that people in strong communities sleep better and live longer. The life-changing ideas in this chapter all encourage people to talk to each other more and build community. At a time when many North Americans report being lonelier and feeling more isolated than ever, community is just what we need.

And did you know that community-building is good for the environment too? Studies show that people who know their neighbors well spend more time close to home. That means less driving. It can mean less shopping, too, if you know your neighbors well enough to share things. Every time we buy something new, a factory uses up natural resources to create more products, so less shopping is definitely good news. Just think—going next door to borrow a paintbrush or a bicycle pump is a kind of environmental activism!

*Cycling can be a healthy and relaxing way to get around. In Copenhagen, Denmark, even downtown traffic doesn't seem so bad when you're pedaling.* AURINKO/DREAMSMTIME.COM

# *My Happy Place*

*One of our young neighbors in particular loves being outside. If the leaves are falling, he's out there raking. When the snow starts, he grabs his shovel. One winter he earned $14 in a few hours because neighbors—some of whom he'd never met before—saw him outside shoveling and asked him to clear their sidewalks. And I can't tell you how many people stopped to admire this snowman, even as it was melting and its nose fell out.*

*Being outside is a great way to meet your neighbors.* GASTÓN CASTAÑO

25

## CHAPTER THREE

# A Potluck of Possibilities

## COME EAT!

How do you make friends when you move from a small village in Ireland to a Canadian city where you don't know anyone? What about inviting everyone on your street over for soup? That's what Grace Gerry did when she moved to Victoria in 2004. It became an annual event; now she knows more than 100 of her neighbors by name, and she's borrowed and lent everything from an egg to a truck.

Mark Lakeman grew up in Portland, Oregon, but he never felt a real sense of community until he spent time in a tiny village on the border between Guatemala and Mexico. After returning home, he decided to build what he had loved so much in that faraway village. He invited everyone on his street over for weekly potlucks. Then the neighbors all decided to create a place outside where they could spend time together. They painted a huge mural on the pavement of the nearest intersection, put up a playhouse and a community bulletin board, built a

*A group of neighbors in Portland, OR, turned a dull, lonely intersection into this unforgettable place called Share-It Square.*
CITYREPAIR.ORG

twenty-four-hour self-serve tea station and created a little lending library. They called their creation Share-It Square. At first city officials were completely against it. One even said, "That's public space—so no one can use it!" But when officials realized that neighbors felt it made city life more enjoyable, they changed local bylaws so more people could create similar squares in other neighborhoods.

## DOWN WITH THE FENCES

Have you heard the old saying "Good fences make good neighbors"? Some people think it means *respect other people's property by staying out.* Others point out that the proverb developed when most people lived on farms, and if you didn't have a good fence, your goats might wander and eat a neighbor's favorite shirt off a clothesline. If you don't have goats, do you really need a fence?

On N Street in Davis, California, neighbors began taking down fences between their properties in 1986. A few years later one of the neighbors converted her house into a "common house," where anyone on the street could use the kitchen or laundry. These days, not a single fence exists along the entire block. Paths connect the yards, and neighbors share everything from meals to fruit trees to a hot tub. Each family decides how much to participate in neighborhood activities, but everyone agrees that it's the lack of fences that makes their neighborhood great.

*Imagine if your local park had its own community oven, like this one in Toronto, ON. What would you and your neighbors bake?*
JUTTA MASON

## BRING US YOUR DOUGH

Can having a park nearby ever be a bad thing? Just over twenty years ago, families living near Dufferin Grove Park in Toronto, Ontario, were wondering exactly that. Teenagers hung out in the park, bringing with them noise and vandalism. At one local meeting, some adults suggested that the only way to clean up the

For centuries, communal ovens have been a valuable community resource. This oven is in a mountain village in Morocco.

neighborhood was for police to arrest the teenagers and throw them in jail.

But one group of families had another idea. What if, instead of keeping teenagers out, they made the park more interesting and invited more people of all ages *in*? Working with the city, they dreamed up a sandpit, a basketball court, a skating rink and eventually two wood-fired public ovens. Why would anyone want brick ovens in a park? To bake bread, of course! Park officials supervised the use of the ovens, and families came from all over the neighborhood to bake their bread. While the dough was in the oven, they chatted with the other neighbors there. Friendships formed, and the area changed from troublesome park to local treasure.

## HUNGRY? HELP YOURSELF!

Public ovens can help strengthen a community...and so can public fridges!

# My Happy Place

*I spend a lot of time in the parking lot of our building. I garden, I tune up our bicycles, and now my family sometimes sits on the new bench to have supper. The last time we were picnicking, a neighbor from down the street came by with a sprouted purple potato. "I found it at the back of my cupboard. I thought you could plant it." I did, and a few months later we had purple potatoes to share.*

*Sprouted potato, anyone?*

When we think of our neighbors, we usually picture the people living in the buildings around us. But many urban communities include folks who live on the street.

Minu Pauline, who runs a popular restaurant in Kochi, India, wanted to help neighbors struggling to survive. When she saw a homeless woman digging through dumpsters, looking for food, Ms. Pauline realized her restaurant could have fed the woman and many others with the leftovers they had thrown away that night. A few days later she set up a fridge out front and encouraged customers to fill it with food that would otherwise wind up in the trash. She calls the fridge *nanma maram* (tree of goodness).

Throughout Argentina, *heladeras sociales* (social fridges) are popping up in front of restaurants or in central plazas, with signs inviting the hungry to take what they need. These fridges both help neighbors and reduce waste. And some fridges stand next to a *perchero social* (social coatrack) where people can get free clothes too.

*Got extra food? In Auckland, New Zealand, you can leave your extras in this community fridge for others to enjoy.*
RAFAEL BEN ARI | DREAMSTIME.COM

# My Happy Place

*A few years ago a friend asked if I wanted to go medlar picking. "What?" I asked. It was November. Nothing edible seemed to be growing anywhere. And what was a medlar anyway? It turns out medlars are a fruit that was popular in the Middle Ages in Europe, and there happens to be a medlar tree at Spring Ridge Commons, a short bike ride from where I live. The commons used to be an empty lot, but a group of neighbors turned it into Canada's largest multilayer community food forest. In other words, volunteers maintain the plants there, and anyone is welcome to harvest. Free food, in the middle of the city! And medlars? They're delicious!*

*Neighbors turned this empty lot into a food forest—a perfect place to chat with friends or pick a fresh snack.*
JENN PLAYFORD

29

## PLAY ME, I'M YOURS!

Are there places in your neighborhood where you see the same people all the time, but no one talks to anyone else? British artist Luke Jerram noticed this happening at his local laundromat. Every weekend he sat with the same people while everyone's laundry spun around in the machines. No one ever spoke a word. He wondered what he could do to change the situation and imagined putting a piano in the space. Years later, when asked to present an art project in Birmingham, England, he decided to try out his idea, and *Play Me, I'm Yours* was born. He installed fifteen pianos in public places in the city for three weeks. Thousands of people played together, laughed and met people they might never have spoken to otherwise. The idea spread, and since then more than 1,500 pianos have been installed in fifty-five cities around the world.

## A WHOLE LOTTA PLATES

The Dutch, with their *woonerven,* are allowed to pull tables and chairs out into the street. But that won't work for everyone. Some of us live in small apartments on busy roads where street eating (also called streating) is not allowed. Are we doomed to eat inside and alone forever?

Not according to artist Hunter Franks. In 2015 he planned a supper for 500 people in the middle of a freeway. He'd heard that the Innerbelt Freeway in Akron, Ohio, would be permanently blocked off to car traffic in 2016, and he wanted to know what people in the city's twenty-two neighborhoods wanted to do with the space instead.

To find out, he talked to families throughout the city and invited them to share a meal on the freeway—blocked off for the event, thank goodness—and brainstorm ideas for the

**NEIGHBORHOOD FACT:**
For generations in Cape Town, South Africa, prejudice separated people based on the color of their skin. Now regular festivals bring people together to celebrate life in their city, break down social barriers and make the streets safer for everyone, all year round.

*The 500 Plates project in Akron, OH, helped neighbors imagine new ways to use this local highway.* SHANE WYNN

*Times Square in New York City, once a noisy, dirty space, is now a lively community gathering place featuring sounds that are much more musical!*
LUKE JERRAM

31

*Snowing and icy outside? Perfect! It's time for a hockey game!*
FATCAMERA/ISTOCK.COM

public space. People suggested creating parks with bike lanes, community gardens and maybe a space for food trucks. After the meal each diner took home a plate printed with one of the many recipes Franks had collected from participants. Franks also gave each neighborhood a table to continue the conversations even closer to home. What a memorable dinner party!

## DESIGNED BY KIDS

What do you get when you mix an abandoned park and a bunch of kids who love the video game *Minecraft*? A new public space for neighbors to enjoy! Lotus Gardens in Mumbai, India, was a brown stretch of dirt with metal playground equipment and hardly any visitors until local kids used *Minecraft* to redesign the whole thing. Now it's a well-loved, colorful public space with grass to picnic on, a new playground and plenty of greenery.

The kid designers were part of a program called Block by Block (which is run by the United Nations Human Settlement Program and Mojang, the developer of *Minecraft*). As part of this program, kids all over the world have used *Minecraft* to make their cities better. Once they've redesigned a space, they take their plans to city council and discuss how to make their plans reality. Imagine watching something you designed in a video game being built in real life!

## HOWDY, FRIEND

Can making space for picnics and potlucks create stronger, more enjoyable neighborhoods? You bet! Cities aren't just for cars anymore. They're for people. In many small ways, we get to decide what our cities look like, and together those small changes create huge ones.

*Neighbors in Victoria, BC, got permission to paint a mural on their street.*
*What a fun way to encourage conversations and slower driving!* DANA HUTCHINGS

# My Happy Place

On our bike ride home from school, my daughter and I pass this street corner. Often we stop to sit and peek at the book box, which always has something new in it—a sign that it's well-loved by many neighbors. One time a man from a nearby construction site pulled up in a bulldozer, hopped out of the cab and grabbed a book before roaring back to work.

*I love this outdoor living room, complete with a book box.* MICHELLE MULDER

# Life in the City

*When kids in Sassari, Italy, challenged local politicians to enjoy the city their way, local politics became extra interesting.*
TAMALACÀ

## POLITICS? KID-APPROVED!

Has the mayor ever asked for your advice? In 2014, during city elections, kids in Sassari, Sardinia, Italy, felt ignored. The adults were all talking about the politicians who would represent them best, but did any of the politicians pay attention to what kids in the city wanted? No! So the young people, with the help of a research group called TaMaLaCà Srl, decided to run their own campaign. They challenged candidates to record themselves experiencing their city the way kids did, by rollerblading or pedaling or inviting passersby to play a street game. As politicians played hard to earn "kid approval," city life suddenly became a lot more fun.

## MAKING A SPLASH

Luckily, you don't need to know politicians to turn your neighborhood into a happy, safe community. Sometimes you just need to enjoy what you already have.

Here in Victoria, British Columbia, the Gorge Waterway was a popular swimming spot at the beginning of the last century. Each summer thousands of people came to swim or paddle, or to picnic on the shore. In the 1930s, though, big industries set up nearby, and local authorities banned swimming because of sewage and industrial waste contamination. Then, in 1994, local residents organized a cleanup effort that soon involved businesses and government. Wildlife that had disappeared—like oysters and salmon—returned to the waterway, and a few years ago people began diving in again too. By splashing around regularly, locals are building a relationship with this special place and encouraging others to do the same. Thanks to caring neighbors, the Gorge has transformed from a toxic dumping ground to a free, natural swimming spot.

*Thanks to a group of dedicated neighbors, the Gorge isn't a polluted waterway anymore. It's a beautiful, natural swimming hole in the middle of the city.* ROYAL BC MUSEUM

# My Happy Place

*Snow day!* SUUSA GEUER

*It doesn't often snow in Victoria, but when it did a few years ago, I took my daughter and our neighbors tobogganing for the first time ever. Together we tromped through the snow to the park, and all the while the kids tried to imagine where we'd be sledding. They knew the park as a quiet, green place with gardens and a petting zoo. They'd never imagined that on a snowy day Beacon Hill transforms into a wild play area packed with people and every imaginable kind of "sled," from scraps of plastic to laundry baskets!*

*Imagine coming across this on a neighborhood stroll! Sisters Lorna and Jill Watt used 6.4 kilometers (4 miles) of yarn to knit this squid tree in San Mateo, CA.* JILL WATT

Don't have a waterway nearby? What about a back alley? In Montreal, Quebec, back alleys stretch throughout the city. A few decades ago they were often gray, smelly with garbage and empty of people. But in the 1990s, groups of neighbors decided to turn their alleyways into community gathering places. They cleaned them up, planted gardens and dragged out tables and chairs. The City of Montreal liked the idea and officially designated these spaces as *green alleys*, even offering to help with planting costs. Now over 250 of these community hubs grace the city, giving kids a place to play and adults a spot to meet, share a meal and enjoy the summer together.

Back alleys aren't just for garbage cans and rats! Potted plants and fresh paint make this inner-city alleyway a welcoming spot to wander. MARKUS JAASKELAINEN/DREAMSTIME.COM

## YARNSTORM!

Picture a long street with tall gray buildings on each side. It's a cloudy day, and people hurry along the sidewalks, heads down…until they reach a bench that's wearing knitted rainbow socks. Or a lamppost wearing a wooly scarf. A woman with a suitcase laughs out loud. A man in a business suit smiles. And a conversation starts.

*Yarnstorming* (sometimes known as *yarn bombing*) is graffiti knitted onto trees, statues, lampposts and other structures around the city. It's illegal in most places because it involves changing public property. But unlike painted graffiti it's easy to remove, and in some places officials choose to leave the colorful tags up because people enjoy the splash of color in an otherwise gray cityscape. One early yarnstormer was Magda Sayeg, who in 2005 knitted a cover for the door handle of her shop in Houston, Texas. She loved the idea of adding a warm, fuzzy touch to the city's gray metal. Other artists use yarn graffiti as a form of "craftivism"—activism through crafts that raise awareness about issues, from women's rights to protecting the environment. Whimsical or challenging, knitstorming gets people talking.

**NEIGHBORHOOD FACT:**
The neighborhood of Fremont in Seattle, WA, includes a bridge. For a long time the area underneath was full of weeds and litter. In 1989 the local neighborhood association decided to turn the area from an eyesore to an asset. That small space is now home to a large sculpture of a troll that's become an important tourist attraction!

Sometimes you can decorate by taking something away—like the dirt on this wall, for example. It's reverse (or clean) graffiti.
YEOWATZUP/WIKIMEDIACOMMONS.ORG

## GIVE ONE, TAKE ONE

Have you ever run out of books to read long before your next visit to the library? Wouldn't it be great if the library were closer— say, right in your own front yard? In Germany in the 1990s, bookcases full of books started appearing in public places, with signs inviting people to take a book and return it later. In 2009, in Hudson, Wisconsin, Todd Bol built a wooden box that looked like a little schoolhouse and filled it with books, in honor of his mother. He placed the box in his yard and invited neighbors to the first Little Free Library. These days, at least 50,000 Little Free Libraries exist in dozens of countries. Folks who live nearby say they've met more neighbors in front of their little libraries than they had in all the years they'd lived on that street!

*Books change landscapes. In Paris, booksellers have been vending along the River Seine since the 1500s, first from wheelbarrows and later from bookstalls like this one.* BENH LIEU SONG/ WIKIMEDIA.ORG

*At the beach in Albena, Bulgaria, and wishing for something to read? You're in luck! This free library offers 6,000 books in 15 languages.* NIKOLAI KORZHOV/DREAMSTIME.COM

BEACH LIBRARY

## SPACE FOR VEGGIES

Imagine if getting vegetables for supper was as easy as wandering through your city, harvesting them here and there. That's what suppertime can look like in the town of Todmorden, England. It started in 2007, when a few friends dreamed up the idea and began planting. Now the footpaths are lined with edible flowers, a local doctor's office is surrounded by fruit trees, and corn grows in front of the police station. Locals harvest and chat with others doing the same. Kids and adults alike are learning to grow their own food, and tourists come from far and wide to marvel at how well this works. The plantings have created jobs, built community and fostered a whole new sense of town pride.

Don't like gardening? Why not head to a farmers' market? That's a sociable way to get local vegetables too. We go to our local farmers' market for the fresh food, the free entertainment and the conversations with the farmers—and also because it feels like a neighborhood festival every Saturday. Unlike grocery

*Mmm. There's no place like a farmers' market for really fresh food. This boy is buying figs in Piombono, Italy.* IMGORTHAND/ISTOCK.COM

# *My Happy Place*

*McCaskill Street is not in my neighborhood, but every time I'm nearby, I visit because the place makes me smile. Neighbors came together to paint this wall, and one project led to another. Now the street has a book exchange, decorated telephone poles, chickens and even chicken crossings marked on the pavement.*

*I love how neighbors transformed an ugly gray wall into a neighborhood icon!*
MAUREEN PARKER

stores, which are usually designed to help customers shop as fast as possible (and spend lots of money), farmers' markets are designed for conversation and participation (and to support local growers). Many markets include kid vendors too, selling everything from crafts to cauliflower. At Aya Community Markets in Washington, DC, for example, students of Eastern Senior High School sell vegetables and herbs that they grow themselves in the school garden. City kids can be farmers too.

## LOOK OUT! HERE WE COME!

Placemaking doesn't always have to change the way a spot looks. Sometimes all it takes is an invitation to get together. In 2010, in Burnie, Tasmania, Australia, neighbors were talking.

*The Billy Project is fun for all ages.* RICK EAVES

They wanted to give their kids the best possible start at life. Then an arts organization called Creature Tales invited primary schoolchildren and their families to meet with residents from an aged-care facility. Their project? To design and build wooden, wheeled "billy carts." (*Billy* is the local word for "child.") Soon kids and adults were parading their carts through the streets, enjoying a sense of community like never before. These days, people of all ages enjoy the annual Billy Project tradition, strengthening connections in the community and supporting kids.

Do you have high-rise apartment buildings in your neighborhood? And have you ever imagined launching a paper airplane from the top floor? Beacon Tower is a high-rise for low-income seniors and people with disabilities in Seattle, Washington. For a long time, folks in the tower kept to themselves, rarely going in and out. Then a few people decided to change that. One day everyone in the neighborhood received an invitation to a Saturday-morning airplane-flying competition on the fifteenth floor of the tower. Some neighbors provided snacks. Others folded airplanes. Local businesses offered prizes for the farthest flier, or the plane that could hit the three-meter (ten-foot) bull's-eye.

## NEIGHBORHOOD FACT:

In big cities the world over you can find people who are trying to "live slower." They shop at farmers' markets, take walks around their neighborhoods and form clubs with other people interested in living slow. One such group in Tokyo, Japan, calls itself The Sloth Club. What a great name!

*Imagine this in front of your local museum. An organization called Archikidz set this up in Sydney, Australia, in 2015 to inspire future citymakers—kids like you!*

VANESSA TROWELL PER JAMES HORAN

*More fun in the museum courtyard! What would cities look like if they were all built with kids in mind?*

VANESSA TROWELL PER JAMES HORAN

By the time neighbors headed outside to retrieve their planes, they weren't strangers anymore, and they'd forever changed the way they viewed their neighborhood too. They'd transformed the place without making any physical changes at all.

## A HELPING HAND

Life in the city is changing, from fast-paced and often lonely to slower and more neighborly. Around the world, people are relying less on cars and more on each other, and the results are stronger neighborhoods and happier neighbors! Want to find out just how cool your neighborhood could become? Here are some ideas to get you started.

### *Be Seen*

One of the best ways to meet your neighbors is simply to show up. If you or your family is outside walking, picnicking, raking leaves, gardening or playing hopscotch, you're much more likely to get to know your neighbors.

*Streets are paved so cars can go faster, but the smooth surface is perfect for street hockey too!*
ROBERT NOEL DE TILLY/SHUTTERSTOCK.COM

*From unused grassy patch to homegrown veggies, sidewalk gardening is a delicious way to meet plenty of neighbors.*
JACKBLUEE/DREAMSTIME.COM

### Explore

Riding your bike or walking is a great way to get familiar with your neighborhood and your neighbors. Make a map and share it with a friend. What interesting details do you notice as you wander around your neighborhood? What's missing, and what could you do about it?

### Think Like an Artist

Take a look at what you've got and put it to good use. Got a front yard? Turn it into a garden. All you've got is a front step? Put flowers next to it. Even apartment dwellers can personalize their neighborhoods. Remember those sidewalk potholes that Steve Wheen transformed with a little creative thinking? Create something that gets people to stop and pay attention.

### Add Books

If your city allows them, creating a book exchange can be a great way to liven up the neighborhood. And you might find some new favorite authors while you're at it!

### Celebrate

What do you love about your neighborhood, and how can you celebrate that? Are the sidewalks perfect for chalk drawing? Would a certain neighbor who plays the saxophone be willing to give a street concert? Folks who appreciate where they live tend to look after it, and that helps others appreciate the place more too.

## HOME SWEET NEIGHBORHOOD

Wherever you live, you've got everything you need to create a stronger community. With a little curiosity, a few smiles and some creativity, you can help turn your neighborhood into a place full of friendly faces…a place that's more fun to live in than ever before!

*In the Victoria, BC, neighborhood of Fernwood, any neighbor can sign up to paint a telephone pole. I love this one by local artist Julie McLaughlin.* JEN CAMERON

*Visiting a book exchange—or starting one of your own—is a great way to meet book-loving neighbors.* EVGENIIAND/DREAMSTIME.COM

# Acknowledgments

**W**hee! I love the acknowledgments section! My first thanks go to my neighbors, who gave me space and encouragement to think about garden boxes and a book exchange for our building parking lot. Thanks to Chris Adams and Mark Weston for introducing me to the concept of place-making and to the Greater Victoria Placemaking Network for the inspiration and practical help!

As I researched, many people were generous with time, information and photos. I'm especially grateful to Maureen Parker, Suusa Geuer, Gastón Castaño, Jen Cameron, Jenn Playford, Teale Phelps Bondaroff, Amy Tompkins, Alan McInnes, Jim Diers, Seth Solomonow, Grace Gerry, Sally Reay, Myrna Canin at Canin Associates, Mike Lanza, Paola Idini at TaMaLaCà Srl, Shani Graham, Vanessa Trowell at Archikidz and Chris Mead at Creature Tales. Thanks also to all the people who were willing to appear in photos in this book.

Several books for adults helped me better understand my subject. Among my favorites were *Deepening Community: Finding Joy Together in Chaotic Times*, by Paul Born; *The Great Neighborhood Book: A Do-It-Yourself Guide to Placemaking*, by Jay Walljasper; *Happy City: Transforming Our Lives Through Urban Design*, by Charles Montgomery; and *Tactical Urbanism: Short-Term Action for Long-Term Change*, by Mike Lydon and Anthony Garcia. Thanks for the inspiration.

And, of course, this book wouldn't have been possible without the fantastic team at Orca Book Publishers. Thanks to Sarah Harvey for excellent editing suggestions, to Vivian Sinclair for careful copy edits and to Jenn Playford for the beautiful design. What a team!

To my family and friends, who have supported me with everything from cups of tea to bags of manure for my boulevard garden, thank you. I'm so grateful to have you all in my life!

# Resources

## Print

Lock, Deborah, Penny Smith, Carrie Love and Margaret Parrish, eds. *Outdoor Crafts: Lots of Fun Things to Make and Do Outside.* London, UK: Dorling Kindersley, 2013.

Vermond, Kira. *Why We Live Where We Live.* Toronto, ON: Owlkids, 2014.

Wheen, Steve. *The Little Book of Little Gardens.* Årsta, Sweden: Dokument Press, 2012.

## Online

**Archikidz:** archikidz.com.au
**Block by Block:** blockbyblock.org
**Little Free Library:** littlefreelibrary.org
**PARK(ing) Day:** parkingday.org
**Play Me, I'm Yours:** streetpianos.com
**Play Streets:** playingout.net
**The Pothole Gardener:** thepotholegardener.com

# Glossary

**bumping place**—a public space where people are likely to see each other, stop and chat

**green alley**—a back alley where local residents have cleaned up, planted gardens and set up street furniture to create a community-gathering place

**Homo sapiens**—the modern human species, which has been around for the past 200,000 years

**inuksuk/inuksuit** (plural)—human-made, stone landmarks, used traditionally by Indigenous peoples of Arctic North America to mark important local places

**mandala**—a diagram or pattern with regular lines or shapes that represents the universe

**Minecraft**—a video game published by Mojang in which players create their own structures with textured 3-D cubes

**nomadic**—living by traveling from place to place rather than settling in one location

**placemaking**—an international movement that aims to change public spaces to draw people together

**playborhoods**—enjoyable, safe streets or residential places where adults encourage kids to play outside

**reverse (or clean) graffiti**—marks made on public or private property by removing dirt, such as drawing a happy face with your fingertip in the dust on a car

**schizophrenia**—a long-term mental disorder that affects how people think, feel and behave and causes them to have trouble figuring out what is real

**street furniture**—objects placed in the street for public use, such as benches or tables

**vandalism**—damages done to public or private property on purpose

**woonerf/woonerven** (plural)—a Dutch word meaning "living street," which refers to a place where people move furniture and plants into the roadway so that cars and trucks slow to walking pace

**yarnstorming/yarn bombing**—covering or decorating public objects with colorful knitting or crocheting

*What would you like your city to be like?* DANA HUTCHINGS

# Index

# Index (continued)